Author:
Ute Schmidt was born in 1965 in Passau, Germany. Already as a child she was surrounded by many animals, especially work and coach horses.
Under the supervision of her stern grandfather, who was a cavalry captain, she learned much about housing, conversation of health and feeding from the very beginning.
She got solid riding lessons in dressage and jumping from the age of ten years.
In 1996 she moved to Hamburg, where she fulfilled her dream of running her own horse riding school.
She lives with her family on a farm in the south-east of Hamburg, where she teaches children and young people on her Friesian horses.

Illustrator:
Mirella Sperling

Cover photo:
Ariane Lange

To go on horseback: level one   ISBN-number: 9783748133483

Translated from german.
Original title: Reitabzeichen 10 ISBN-Nr.: 9783734761102

Other publications in german language:
Reitabzeichen 4   ISBN – Nummer 9783756215188
Reitabzeichen 5   ISBN - Nummer 9783746092966
Reitabzeichen 6   ISBN - Nummer 9783739243177
Reitabzeichen 7   ISBN - Nummer 9783739207667
Reitabzeichen 8   ISBN - Nummer 9783738637441
Reitabzeichen 9   ISBN - Nummer 9783734793226
Longierabzeichen 5   ISBN - Nummer 9783741237454
Pferdeführerschein Reiten ISBN - Nummer 9783751984218
Pferdeführerschein Umgang ISBN - Nummer 9783750437210
Bodenarbeit Stufe   ISBN - Nummer 9783746050133
Trainerassistent   ISBN – Nummer 9783750435209

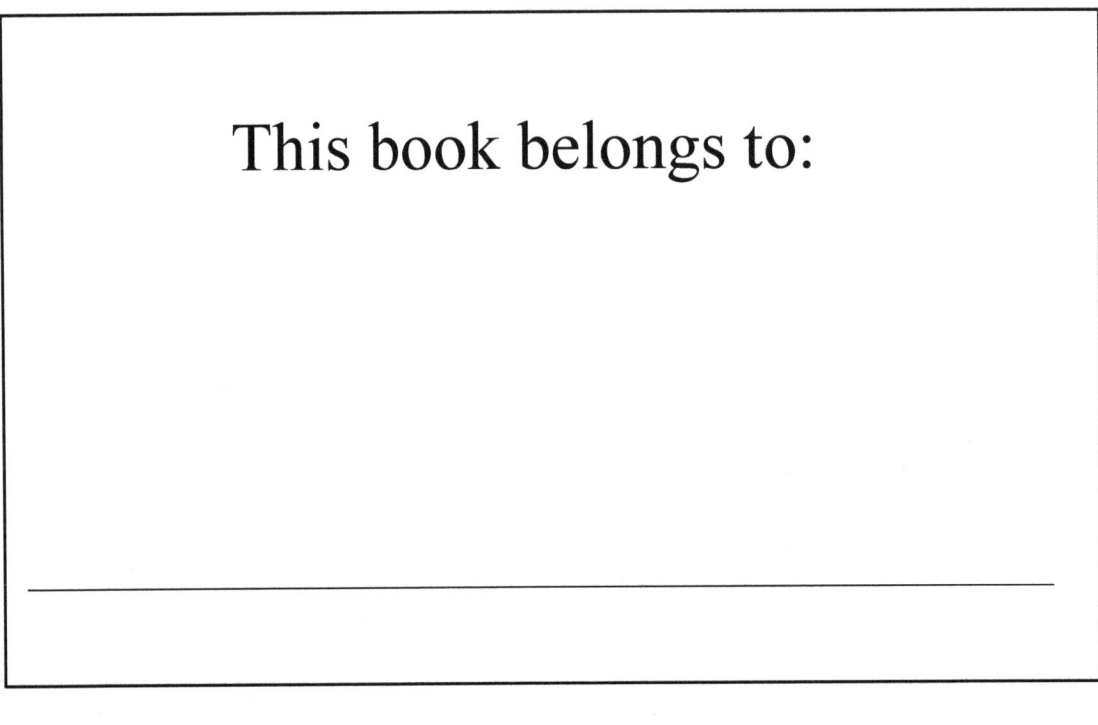

This book belongs to:

Table of contents

Chapter 1: How to avoid accidents

🐴 Do you need a helmet?	☐ A helmet is obligatory when riding! Also when dealing with the horse it is highly recommended, because you can get hurt.
🐴 What kind of shoes do you need when dealing with horses?	☐ Horses are large and heavy. Solid shoes only.
🐴 What do you do first when approaching a horse?	☐ You address it and wait until your horse looks kindly at you.
🐴 What do you have to consider when you lead a horse behind another one?	☐ Make sure that adequate space remains between horses. Recommended are two horses.
🐴 Is it possible to scream and rage in the presence of horses?	☐ Horses are flight animals. Therefore always deal with horses in a peaceful and quiet tone.

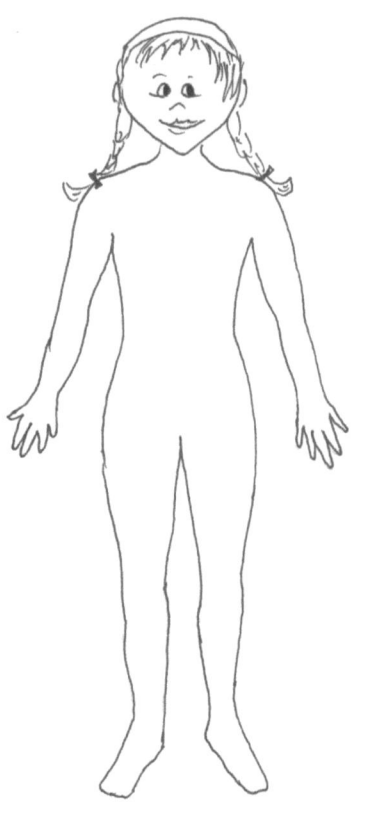

What is missing here?

Grab the crayons and paint the missing outfit.

Chapter 2: How horses talk to you

🐴 What does a horse express when it lays back its ears and how do you react ?	☐ The horse is grumpy. You may not be able to get too close. Get help and be very careful.
🐴 How do you recognize that your horse is resting?	☐ The head is hanging down and one of the hind legs is bent.
🐴 How can you approach a dormant horse?	☐ Call its name before you approach, so that it notices you and does not get startled.
🐴 What does it mean when your horse pricks its ears forward and looks at you?	☐ Your horse is interested and would like to do something with you.
🐴 What does a highly lifted tail mean?	☐ Your horse is very excited. You have to soothe it and be very careful.
🐴 What does it mean when your horse puts its tail between the legs?	☐ The horse is scared and must be reassured. You have to be careful.
🐴 Why is it not allowed to shout at or beat a scared horse?	☐ This way the situation will only get worse. Talk to it sothingly and it will trust you.
🐴 Why shouldn't you feed your horse with treats?	☐ Your horse will want to have more treats over the time and if it doesn't get them, it will start to bite or hit with ist hooves.

Label the mood of the horses

☐

☐

☐

☐

Chapter 3: How to get your horse from the pasture

🐴	What do you do if you want to get your horse from the pasture?	☐	Speak in a clear and quiet tone and watch how your horse reacts.
🐴	Why is addressing the horse so important?	☐	Attract the horses's attention and avoid getting it startled or hurting itself or others.
🐴	From which side do you approach the horse?	☐	Always from the front, never from behind.
🐴	How do you get a horse out of its loose-box?	☐	Get it used to come to the door so you do not have to get inside the box.

Chapter 4: How you tack up the halter

What should you take care of before you put on the halter?	☐ First sort out the halter. Then approach the horse`s head from the left side.
What do you do with the lead rope?	☐ You put the lead rope over your shoulder, so it does not hang on the ground and you have your hands free.
Where is the proper place to put the head collar and how do you secure it?	☐ The noseband is put approx. 4 fingers width above the nostrils and is closed with the snap hook when everything is straight.

Chapter 5: How you lead your horse safely

◼ How do I lead a horse?	☐ Always at the level of the horse's head.
◼ What do you have to take care of when you hold then lead rope?	☐ Never wrap the lead rope around the hand, wrist or fingers, because the horse could drag you away.
◼ How do you hold the lead rope?	☐ One hand holds tightly on to the panic snap, the other holds the end of the rope.
◼ Where are you allowed to lead your horse with a halter?	☐ Only in the stable area, not on the road.
◼ How can I stop my horse?	☐ Shortly pull on the lead rope and say with a calm voice: „Stop"!

🐴 How do you lead a horse using a bridle?	☐ Remove the reins from the horse's neck. Use both hand to hold the reigns: One just behind the snaffle rings and the other hand further away.
🐴 What should you take care of when the horse is saddled?	☐ The stirrups should not hang down loosely so the horse does not get caught on doorknobs or the stirrups beating against the belly.
🐴 What do you do when the horse is uncooperative?	☐ Do not pull the horse behind you. By clicking your tongue you can request the horse to go faster.
🐴 Where do you look at when you lead your horse?	☐ Always look forward, so that you do not stumble or fall.
🐴 What do you do when the horse is going too fast for you?	☐ You calm it down with your voice and try to slow it down by briefly pulling on the reins.
🐴 How do you lead the horse in turns?	☐ Depending on which side you lead your horse make sure you push away the horse from you. If you're leading left, turn to the right and vice versa. Otherwise it can run over your heels. Ensure there is enough space for your turns.

Chapter 6: Now we tie up the horse

🐴 Can you still use a frayed lead rope or a broken halter?	☐ No, because both have to endure quite a bit.
🐴 Why is this so important?	☐ Because horses are very strong and they could easily tear themselves away. This is very dangerous for the horse and for you.
🐴 What is a panic snap and why do you need it?	☐ It can be opened very simply to free a horse in danger fast and secure.
🐴 What ist the most secure way to fasten a horse?	☐ On both sides.
🐴 At which height above the floor do you have to fasten your horse?	☐ On height of the point of shoulder height.
🐴 How long should the tie rope be?	☐ So long that the horse can still move around but cannot not step on it. If it is too short the horse can become nervous.

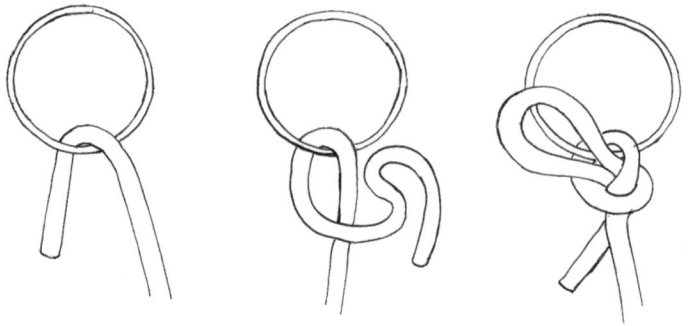

🐴 Can you tie a horse on to the rods of a loose-box?	☐ Only when there is no other horse inside this loose-box. Never tie the horse to the door because it is not strong enough.
🐴 What danger could occur when a horse is in this box?	☐ By fighting your horse may be hurt or tear itself off.
🐴 What must be taken into account, when several horses are in the stable lane?	☐ Make sure there is enough distance: neither should the heads nor the hooves come too close to each other.

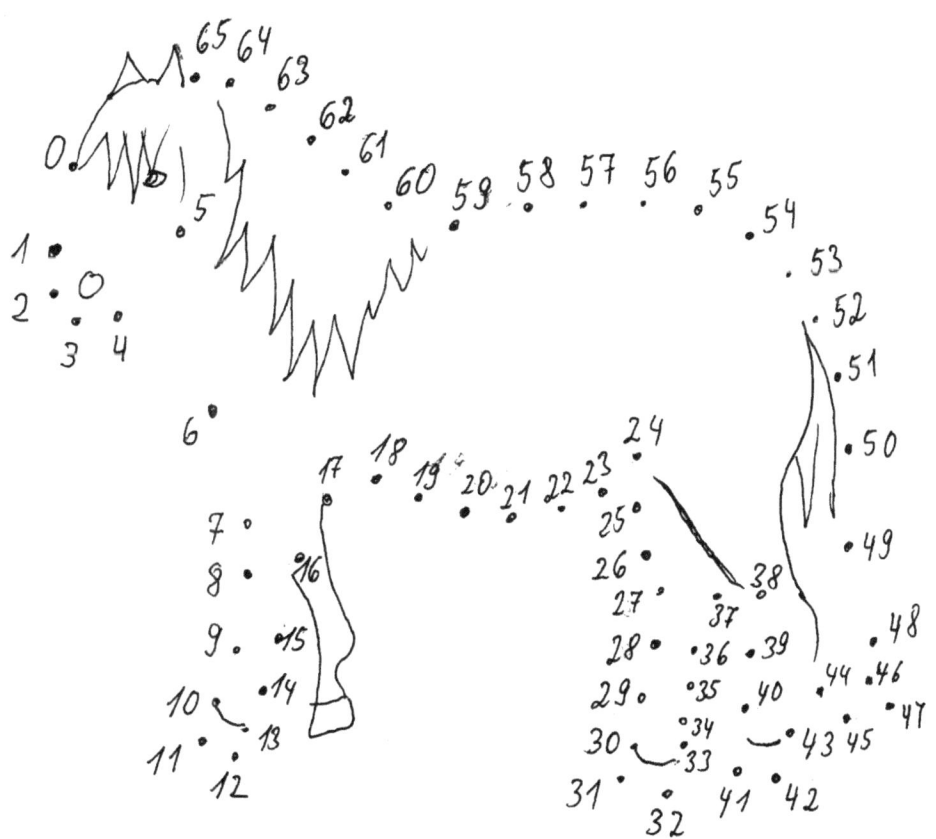

Chapter 7: Now we groom the horse

🐴 What do you need to groom your horse?	☐ Curry comb, dandy brush, body brush, hoof pick, hoof grease and paper towels.
🐴 How long should the grooming take ?	☐ Grooming may not take too long, because your horse may get bored and make nonsense.
🐴 Can you groom the horse in the loose-box?	☐ No, because there is a risk that you will be pressed against the wall. Also the dirt gets into the bedding or feeding.
🐴 Where is the best place to groom the horse?	☐ In the fresh air.
🐴 How often do you groom your horse and why?	☐ Once a day. This way you can detect injuries or illnesses in time. Also you get used to each other. And the horse should look pretty and feel good by your grooming.
🐴 What ist the groming sequence?	☐ Clean from front to back and top to bottom.

Label the grooming kit!

🐴 What do you use first?	☐ The curry comb. All body parts of the horse can be groomed thoroughly in circles avoiding areas where bones are close to the skin. With this you help release coarse dirt as well as loose hair.
🐴 What's next?	☐ After the grooming take the body brush in the other hand. If you're standing on the left side of the horse, you put it into your left hand, and vice versa. The fure should be brushed straight in long and gentle strokes.
🐴 How do you clean body brush and curry comb?	☐ Use the body brush against the curry comb in the direction of the finger tips. The curry comb should be tapped on the floor.
🐴 What follows the brushing of the fur?	☐ The head, next the mane and then the tail.
🐴 How do I clean the horse`s face?	☐ With a soft brush, gently clean the face. Clean the eyes, nostrils and mouth with a paper towel if necessary.

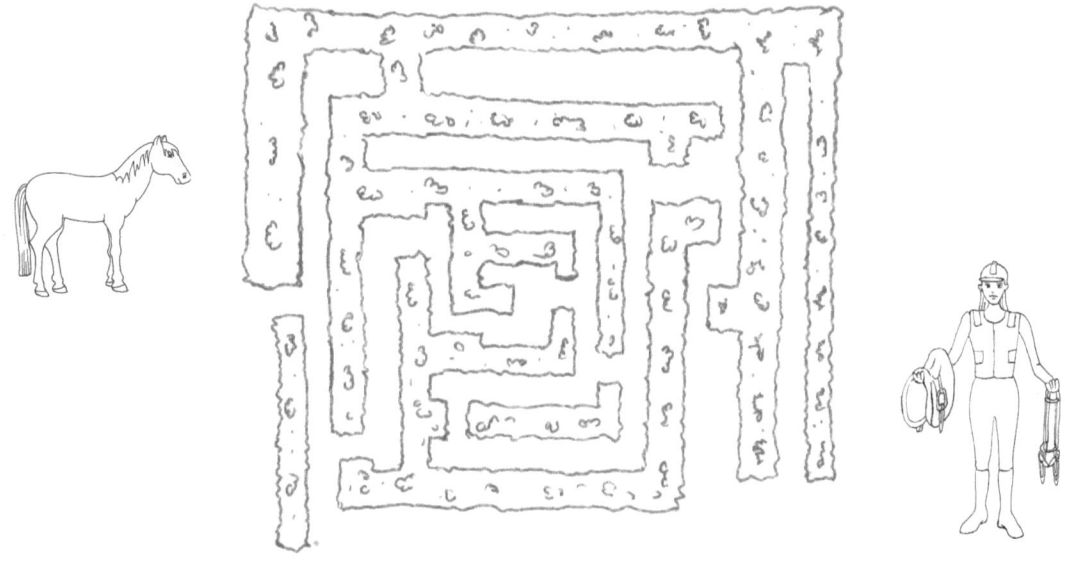

Chapter 8: Neat long hair

🐴 How does one maintain the tail and mane?	☐ The mane and tail needs mane spray to untie knots. This way you can clean the mane and tail with a mane brush easily. Horses with a small tail may not need brushing. Instead the tail hair should be untangled. The tail should be washed every now and then using horse shampoo.
🐴 How to untangle the tail?	☐ You put the tail in one hand and pull out single hair strands with the other hand. Untangling can be very time consuming.

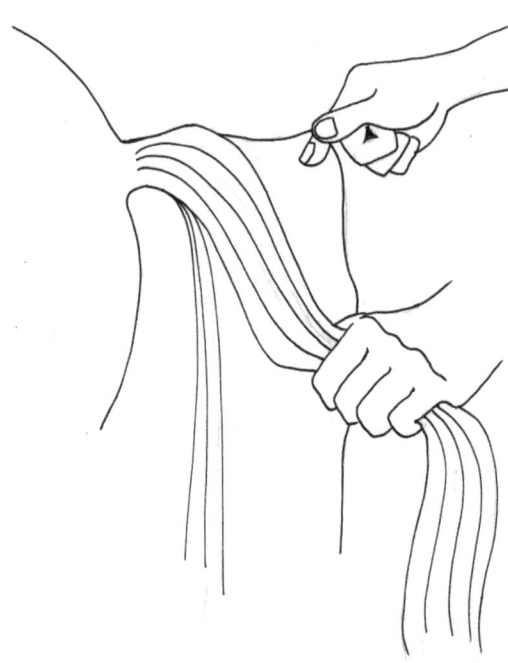

🐴 What do you have to consider before lifting the hooves?	☐ Make sure that there is enough space and no one is in the way in case the horse kicks out.
🐴 How do you lift a hoof ?	☐ Speak to the horse, guide your hand down along the leg and grip the hoof joint with both hands. You can support the horse's leg on your own leg. After cleaning put the hoof down again carefully so that your horse does not get hurt.
🐴 And now hoof care!	☐ First you clean only from the outside using a scrubbing brush and then carefully scrape without scratching the hoof. Here you can see a triangle in the middle of the foot, where you need to be especially careful. It is called frog. When it has been hot and sunny for a long time moisten the hoof and grease thoroughly.

Pearl Necklace

Solve the puzzles!
1 white horse
2 utility to groom the horse
3 this loves the horse to eat
4 put it over the horse's head
5 the fly flap of the horse
6 horse's foot
7 a brown horse
8 a horses mouth

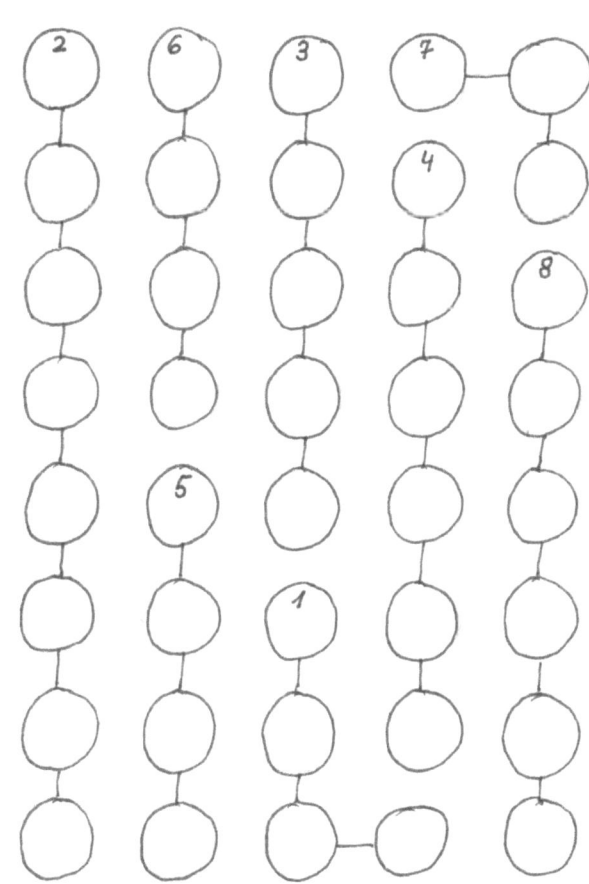

Chapter 10: The saddle

🐴 Enumerate the components of a saddle!	☐ Gullet, seat, flap, stirrups and girth. You will learn more items in the next book.
🐴 What in particular should be consider with the gullet ?	☐ The saddle should not press down on the withers.
🐴 What is the function of the saddle pad?	☐ The saddle pad absorbes sweat and should be cleaned in the washing machine.
🐴 What is an important aspect of the stirrups?	☐ They should be big and heavy so that you can catch them with your foot again when it is lost during riding. Also you should easily get out when tumbling.

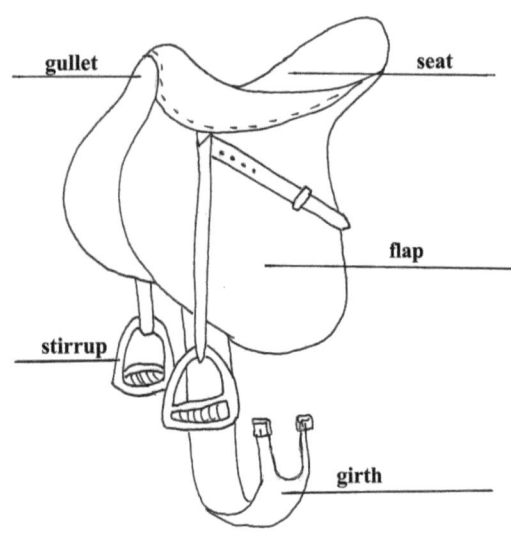

Label the saddle parts

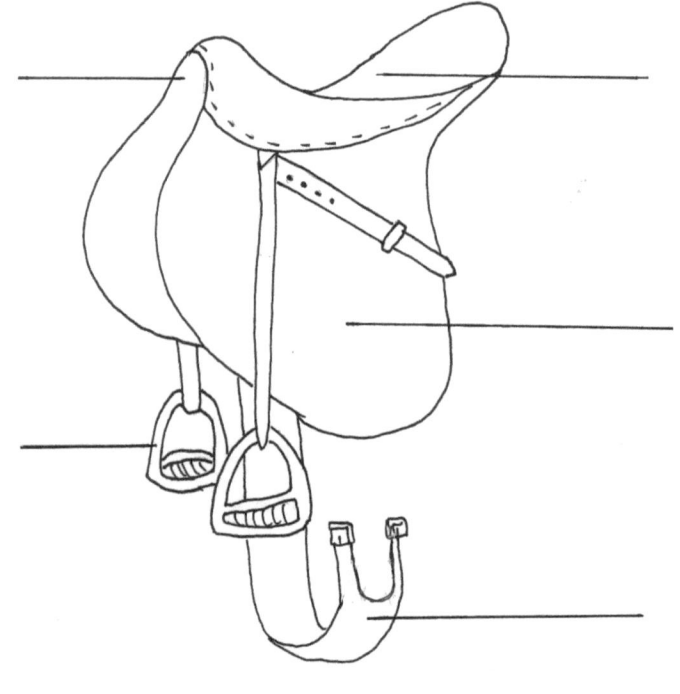

🐴 What do you mount first, saddle or bridle?	☐ The horse gets saddled first. Then put on the bridle.
🐴 How do you begin saddling?	☐ Put the saddle on the left arm, attract the horse's attention and put the saddle up gently and as far to the front as possible. Then push it back into position so that the fur is kept smooth.
🐴 How do you finish saddling ?	☐ Make sure that the saddle pad has no wrinkles and is not lying on the withers. If everything is fine fasten the girth gently.
🐴 What is the correct position of the saddle ?	☐ There has to be a hand-width space between the horse's elbow and the front edge of the girth.

Chapter 11: The bridle

🐎 Name some parts of a bridle!	☐ Browband, noseband, throat lash, bit, flash, reins. You will learn more in the next level.
🐎 How do you tack up a bridle ?	☐ First untangle the bridle and put the reins over the neck of the horse. Then push the bit into the mouth and move the bridle over the ears.
🐎 What's next now?	☐ Put all parts carefully into order and begin closing the bridle. First close the noseband - two fingers should fit between the nose-line and the noseband. Then close the locking strap - just like the noseband. In the end you close the throat lash - a fist must still fit between throat lash and neck.

Label the bridle!

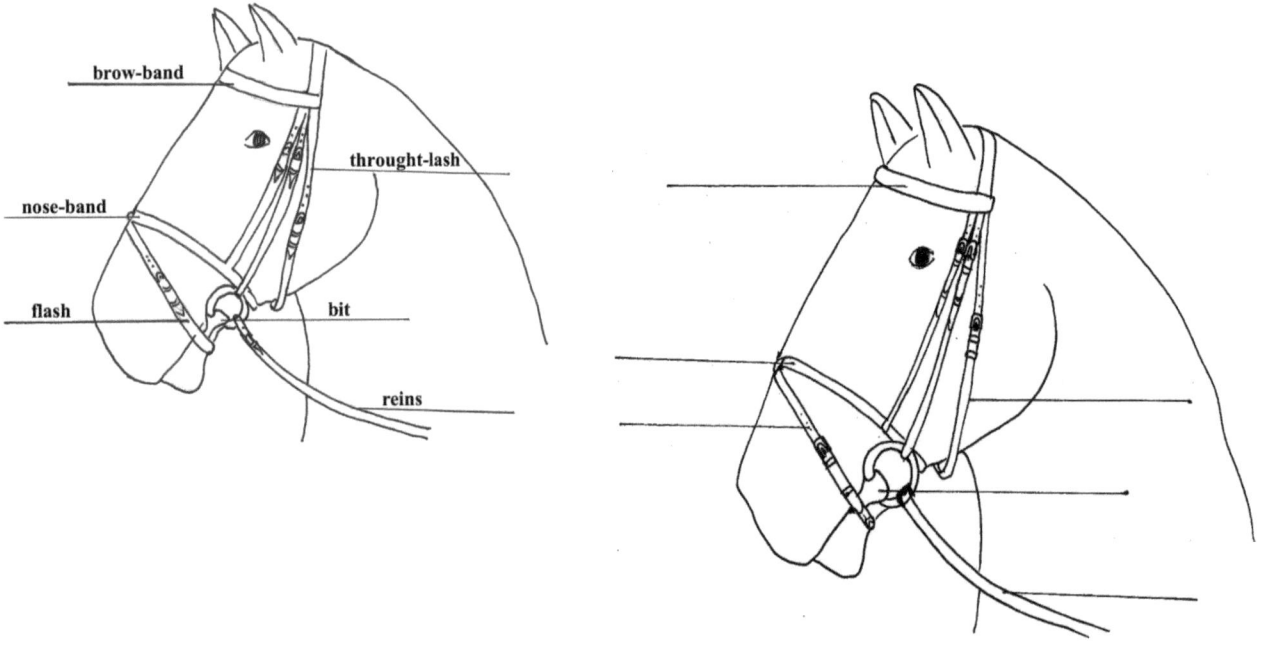

brow-band

throught-lash

nose-band

flash   bit

reins

Chapter 12: The body parts of the horse

1	ears	2	forelock
3	eyes	4	nostrils
5	muzzle	6	mane
7	withers	8	point of shoulder
9	neck	10	back
11	croup	12	tail hair
13	belly	14	hoof

Try to label the body parts !

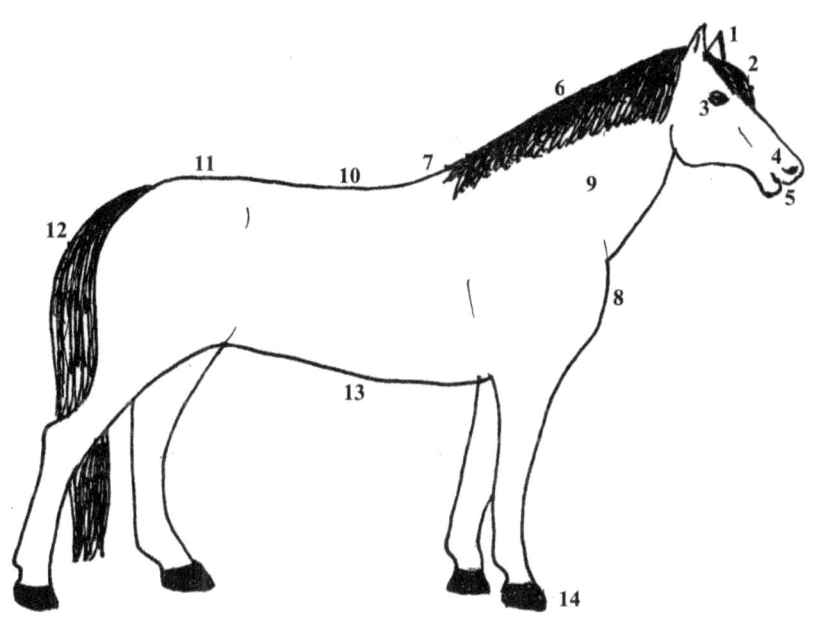

1		2	
3		4	
5		6	
7		8	
9		10	
11		12	
13		14	

Chapter 13: Horses are colorful

🐴 What are the most common colors of horses?	☐ Grey, black, bay and chestnut.
🐴 What is the difference between a bay and a chestnut?	☐ The bay has a brown top coat and black long hair. The chestnuts coat and long hair are of the same color.
🐴 What is a skewbald?	☐ A horse with irregularly shaped spots on the coat, which can have all possible colors.

Paint the horses with their correct coloring!

Bay

Grey

Black

Chestnut

Skewbald

Chapter 14: Rules on the riding arena

🐴 Why should you be acquainted with the rules of a outdoor arena?	☐ To avoid accidents in the arena when everybody rides as he likes to.
🐴 What do you have to keep in mind when entering or leaving the outdoor arena ?	☐ Before you open the door or enter the arena make sure you don`t disturbe other riders.
🐴 Where should you put your horse in order to mount or dismount?	☐ The best position is in the middle of one of the two circles because there is less traffic.
🐴 Where is the track?	☐ Always outside along the arena. There are 3 tracks.
🐴 Who has the right of way in the whole arena ?	☐ Always the one who rides counter-clockwise. You recognize it by the fact that your left hand points to the center of the arena. In the walk you leave the track for faster riders.
🐴 What must you consider when dodging?	☐ Choose a large margin of safety, so no other rider gets endangered or touched by the whip.
🐴 What should you keep in mind when more than three riders are in the arena?	☐ Everyone should ride in the same direction to avoid accidents.

Chapter 15: Now I sit properly on the horse

🐴 How do you correctly position your bottom on a horse?	☐ You put your weight evenly on both sides and try to make yourself heavy.
🐴 How do you position your head and upper body?	☐ Always look straight forward between the ears of your horse. Your upper body and your back should be upright.
🐴 How do you position arms and hands?	☐ Your arms lie gently on the upper body. Your hands enfold the reins tightly while the thumbs must be on top like a little roof. Your hands must not rest on the horse . Hold them upright.
🐴 How do I position the feet?	☐ Your heel should be the lowest point. Your ankle should be loose. Also the tips of your toes should point in the direction of the horse's mouth.
🐴 How can you make it easy to sit calm on the horse?	☐ By joining the rhythm of the horse`s steps with your waist. In this way you order your horse to go forward.
🐴 Why is it so important to sit calmly on the horse?	☐ This way you learn step by step to use your arms and legs independently to give the necessary aids to your horse.

Chapter 16: Now I know the aids

🐴 What are aids?	☐ Aids are the language in which riders and horses communicate without talking to each other.
🐴 What kinds of aids do you know?	☐ There are weight aids, leg aids and rein aids. The weight and leg aids are much more important than the rein aids.
🐴 Which of them are you used to move your horse foreward?	☐ The leg aids and the weight aids.

🐴 There are two kinds of rein aids. Which ones do you know?	☐ Asking rein aid and yielding rein aid.
	  Note:
	    After the asking rein aid the yielding rein aid is following immediatly.

🐴 Do you give all aids one after another or at the same time?	☐ Your horse understands you best if you use the aids at the same time. But that must be practiced.
🐴 What is a full halt?	☐ At a full halt the horse always stops. Give an asking rein aid, press your legs on the belly and shift your weight in the saddle. Then give the yielding rein aid and your horse will stop.

How does the horse find the carrot?

Chapter 17: Riding figures

🐴 What are figures?	☐ Figures are exercises where you will learn to steer your horse along a given path and drive the horse forward.
🐴 What is the benefit of the dressage letters at the sides of arena?	☐ The letters are for guidance if you want to ride figures properly.
🐴 How can you remember these dressage letters ?	☐ You can remember it with the saying: **All King Edwards Horses Can Make Big Fences.**
🐴 Where is the center-line?	☐ The center-line runs along dressage letters A and C.
🐴 Which school figures do you know ? **Label the four drawings.**	☐ They are named: • to go large • one-loop serpentine on the long side • circle • change of rein on long diagonal

Chapter 18: And after work...

🐎 What should you consider after riding?	☐ You need to clean the horse where it has sweated with a moist sponge and brush the fur straight. The hooves also should be scratched out. If the hooves are dried out, wet them all around and grease them.
🐎 What should you do, when it is hot outside and the horse is sweating after work?	☐ The horse should be showered and wiped off with a sweat scraper. You should not shower your horse on the head and the belly. Again brush smoothly and practice good hoof care!
🐎 What should you do after grooming the horse?	☐ After the horse has been well supplied, it has earned a nice, welcoming loose-box, where a reward is waiting for it.
🐎 What should happen to the bridle ?	☐ The bit has to be thoroughly cleaned. If the bridle has become wet it must be dried well.
🐎 What do you do with the saddle ?	☐ The saddle pad should be hung up to the airing. If stirrup and girth have become dirty, they should be removed and cleaned. If the saddle has become wet it must be dried.

Chapter 19: 1 x 9 of horse lovers

1 x 1	☐ Horses need us. We must care for them.
1 x 2	☐ Horses need grooming, light and air, forage, exercise and a friend.
1 x 3	☐ The horse's health is more important than prices and cups.
1 x 4	☐ No matter whether young, old, big, small, cute or ugly - we deal every horse equally well.
1 x 5	☐ In other countries people ride differently - we should look at these and learn from them.
1 x 6	☐ Horses feel our moods. If we are impatient or uncontrolled, they also will be. That's why we have to learn to deal with them patiently and kindly.
1 x 7	☐ Horses are very different. What one horse can do, another can`t. Therefore you should not force a horse to do something what it cannot archieve.
1 x 8	☐ As a rider you can still learn more. So does the horse.
1 x 9	☐ Horses do not get as old as human beings. If our horse is seriously ill, we must redeem it. The veterinarian will put down our horse. It then gets to horses' heaven.

Chapter 20: How to feed a horse

🐎 Why should you not ride your horse right after feeding it?	☐ Horses have a very small stomach. If you want to ride, you have to wait for one to two hours so that your horse gets no abdominal pain - called colic.
🐎 How often should you feed a horse?	☐ Your horse should get feeding amounts several times, at least three times a day.
🐎 When do you feed the horse?	☐ Morning, noon and evening. Feed the largest portion in the evening because the horse has more time to digest. You always feed at the same hour and make it is quiet.
🐎 What kind of forage is there?	☐ Hard feed, succulent feed und dry feed.
🐎 What is dry feed and why is it so important for horses?	☐ Hay and straw are dry feed. Our horse needs dry feed to avoid abdominal pain. The horse takes much time to eat and does not get bored in its loose-box.
🐎 What kind of feed does belong to succulent feed?	☐ Grass, apples, carrots and turnips. Its a nice change in the feeding routine.
🐎 How many times a day do horses need to ger water?	☐ At least three times a day. It is easier if you have a automatic water-bowl for the horse.
🐎 How much water do horses drink ?	☐ Approx. three up to five buckets full of water. These are about 30-50 litres. Less in winter, more in summer when it is hot.

Chapter 21: The leather care

🐴 How are saddle and bridle stored?	☐ Always in a tack room, because the leather gets busted under the dust of the stable. And the horses could nibble off the leather when it is in reach.
🐴 Why is care so important ?	☐ The equipment is expensive and must be well taken care for, so that it does not break. Rough leather can tear, which can be very dangerous.
🐴 How do I clean the leather materials ?	☐ First you disassemble the leather items. All buckles must be opened. Then you clean the leather from both sides with a moist sponge and the saddle soap. Then the leather is being relubricated with leather grease using a flannel from both sides. The seat should not be greased!
🐴 How are the other items looked after?	☐ The saddle pad should be washed regularly in a washing machine. Stirrups and the girth are cleaned with water and a brush.

Search for the words:

x	h	s	g	b	r	i	d	l	e
f	o	r	e	l	o	c	k	n	s
a	o	e	h	a	y	t	s	m	t
p	v	g	j	c	q	t	r	o	t
p	e	r	o	k	y	b	a	y	ö
l	s	a	d	d	l	e	t	a	w
e	s	s	c	d	v	g	l	e	b
d	k	s	l	s	w	d	g	h	j

HOOVES
BLACK
BRIDLE
SADDLE
FORELOCK
GRASS
HAY
APPLE
BAY
TROT

Proposal for a dressage test

C – A	Entrance in medium walk, to go large
A	Turn to centerline
X	Halt and salute
X - C	Move off in medium walk, left hand
A	Turn to centerline, four loop serpentines, then right hand
M	Change of rein on long diagonal
F – M / H - K	Trot on long sides, sitting trot
F	Change of rein on long diagonal
M – F / K - H	Trot on long sides, rising trot
C, M, B, F	Full halt at the dressage letters, then move up
A	Move off in medium walk, give the reins
H	Take up the reins
A	Line up at the centerline
X	Halt and salute

Draw the dressage test into the arena!

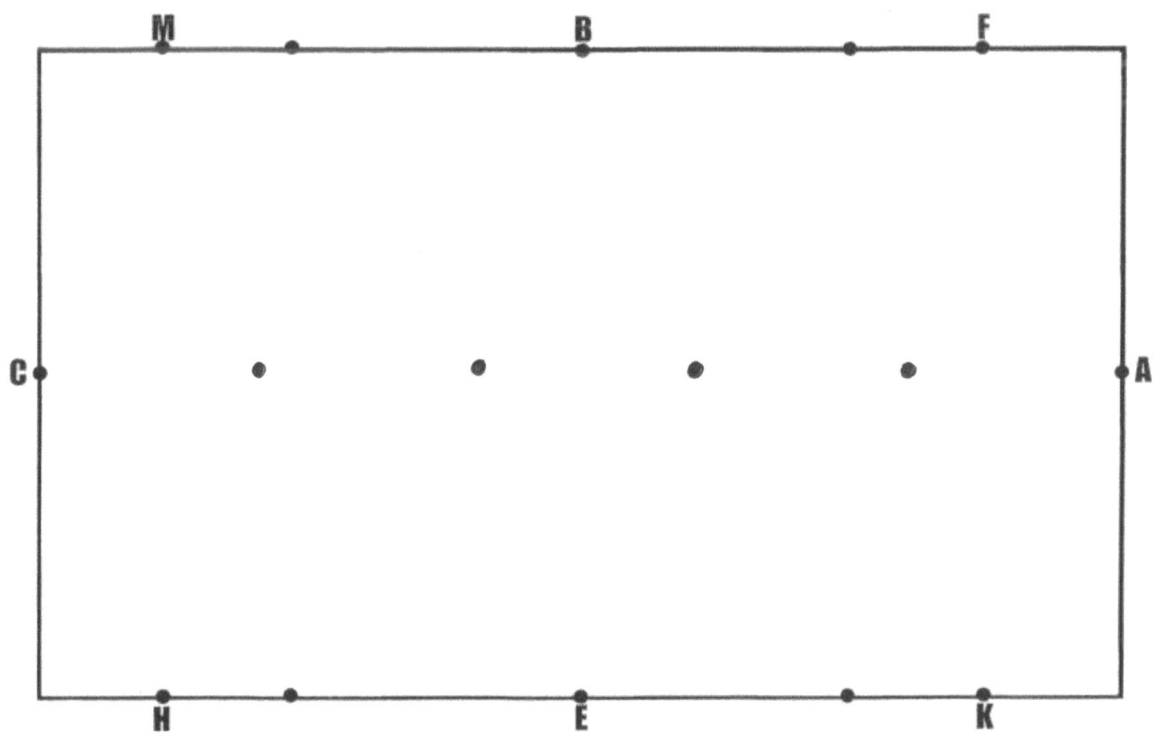

Practical tests

for _____

Ground work: passed on:

I know how to approach to the horse	
I can get the horse out of the loose-box	
I can tack on the halter	
I can lead my horse and stop it	
I can tie up my horse	
Security in the stable lane is important, because...	
I know how to turn the horse	

The horse: passed on:

Make my horse shine	
Shining tail and mane	
Shining hooves	
I can saddle my horse	
I can tack the bridle on	
I know what to do after work	

Practical riding: passed on:

Walk on the lunge - no problem	
Trot on the lunge - no problem	
Department step riding	
Department sitting trot is hard	
Department rising trot is even more difficult	

Theoretical test

for _____

Topic	page	passed on:
How to avoid accidents	4	
How horses talk to you	5	
How to get your horse from the pasture	6	
How you tack up the halter	7	
How you lead your horse safely	8/9	
Now we tie up the horse	10/11	
Now we groom the horse	12/13	
Neat long hair	14	
Shiny hooves	15	
The saddle	16/17	
The bridle	18	
The body parts of the horse	19	
Horse are colourful	20	
Rules on the riding arena	21	
Now I sit properly on the horse	22	
Now I know the aids	23	
Riding figures	24	
And after work...	25	
1 x 9 of horse lovers	26	
How to feed a horse	27	
The leather care	28	

Imprint

Ute Schmidt
Hamburg

Contact
E-Mail: books@tschmidt.de

Producing and publishing:
BoD – Books on Demand, Norderstedt, Germany
ISBN-Nummer: 9783748133483

FSC
www.fsc.org

MIX
Papier aus verantwortungsvollen Quellen
Paper from responsible sources
FSC® C105338